Unleash Your Inner Entrepreneur:

Unlock Your Business In 8 Simple steps

MOGOMOTSI LEKOKO

ASHWIN SUNASSEE

ISBN: 978-1-8381386-7-7

Contribution by: Andrea Corbett

Edited by: Walker Kornfeld

Get access to your Trello Board @ https://forms.gle/V5bHCaRFEoNbd4xu5

Table of Contents

1

WELLBEING AND WHY IT'S IMPORTANT

Success Mindset for Entrepreneurs

Every small business owner and entrepreneur is in a relentless pursuit to grow their business. They usually do this by looking at external methods, such as outsourcing key tasks like accounting, or installing automation software to take care of mundane tasks so they can focus on more important matters. They may try out new marketing tactics or sales strategies as well.

All of these external measures can make a tremendous difference in your business. But we often forget about internal factors such as beliefs, attitudes,opinions and habits of thinking, all of which have a massive impact on the success of your business. In fact, these internal factors are instrumental in determining it.

What is Mindset?

The concept of mindset was first formulated and popularized by Stanford

University psychologist Carol Dweck. Dweck's research focuses on the field of achievement and success. Her theory states that factors like intelligence and ability, while important, do not guarantee success. Rather, our mindset and our beliefs about our abilities play a key role in fuelling or dampening our success.

All of us know someone who is incredibly intelligent or gifted but somehow never realized their potential. Think of the valedictorian who ended up working a dead- end job or the gifted athlete who gave up a sports scholarship in order to stay closer to home. These people seem stunted somehow and it's a great shock that they don't pursue their potential. It's easy to see that there's something holding them back that have nothing to do with ability or talent.

In the simplest terms, your mindset is a collection of beliefs. It includes beliefs about basic qualities like your intelligence, talents, and personality.

For example, you might have a certain view regarding your own intelligence. You may believe that you aren't 'smart' because you didn't perform well in school, as it's widely believed that school performance equals intelligence. This may manifest itself in thoughts like, 'I'm not smart because I didn't get good grades.

Only smart people are successful. Therefore my business will never be successful.' This negative thinking ignores the fact that intelligence means so much more than just school performance, and that many who did poorly in school went on to be great successes in their field.

Or you may have a negative mindset about your talents. You may be asked to speak at an event that could lead to great opportunities for your business, but you decline because of a self-limiting belief. You may think, 'I'm not a good public speaker. When I presented my thesis in college, I choked. I couldn't remember certain words and I was too nervous to perform well. I'm just not a public speaker.' However, public speaking is a skill that anyone can learn through practice.

Whether conscious or unconscious, this negative mindset directly impacts your success. On the other hand, a positive mindset can help you activate your potential and reach heights of prosperity and achievement you never imagined possible.

The Inner Critic

Your mindset and its beliefs can be totally unconscious. It's not always easy to identify them, but that's what must be done in order to draw them out. For many people, a negative mindset manifests itself as an 'inner critic'. This is an inner voice or private conversation that occurs in your mind on continuous repeat mode behind your conscious thoughts.

Your inner critic tells you that you're wrong, you're bad at the task at hand, you're inadequate, or you lack the worth you see in other successful individuals. It acts as a judge, condemning you to failure at every turn.

Some people are aware of this inner critic while others aren't. Even if you're aware of this voice, you may be at a loss for how to deal with it. Many people believe that the inner critic is themselves talking. They mistakenly identify with it and this is why it's so good at sabotaging your life and thwarting your chances for success.

All of us have an inner critic. The first step to cultivating a mindset for success is to become aware of these negative thoughts and the impact they have on you.

Once you've become aware of this inner voice, you've taken the first step toward releasing its grip on you.

The wonderful thing about mindset is that it's malleable. It can be developed and evolved. The negative mindset that's holding you back was shaped through experiences in the past and learned habits of thinking. Through even the smallest shifts in awareness and thinking habits, you can make profound changes and eventually take control of your mindset and steer it toward positivity and success.

Growth vs. Fixed Mindsets

A fixed mindset means that you believe that your character, intelligence and other abilities are static — that they are fixed parts of who you are and can never be changed.

A key characteristic of a fixed mindset is the need some people feel to constantly prove themselves. Since you only have a set amount of intelligence, personality, morality and so on, you need to constantly prove yourself. People with fixed mindsets often become consumed with proving themselves in class, at their jobs or in their relationships.

This constant proving of yourself to others comes from the need to confirm your existing intelligence, talents and abilities. This arises out of a concern over whether you will look smart or stupid, be accepted or rejected, succeed or fail. In this case, the individual with the fixed mindset is overly concerned with the static labels they have come to identify with themselves, such as 'intelligent, gifted, talented' and so on.

A growth mindset is one wherein an individual sees character, intelligence and abilities as always developing and evolving. Unlike the fixed mindset, a growth mindset doesn't compel you to constantly prove yourself because you know that you can change and grow with experience and practice. Your qualities aren't fixed.It doesn't matter if others see that you lack perfect qualities because all of us are always growing and learning.

A key element to success in any field is the willingness and desire to learn new things, grow and accept change. This is why a growth mindset is strongly associated with success.

Which Mindset Do You Have?

In order to understand where you fall on the spectrum of growth vs. fixed mindset,please complete the provided assessment, in which you'll rate yourself on a variety of statements.

This assessment is based on the work of Carol Dweck. The quiz was originally written for educational settings. While it is not scientifically validated, it offers a good benchmark of where you stand in terms of fixed vs. growth mindset. Check the link below:

https://www.londonacademyoit.co.uk/blog/interactive-quiz-fixed-vs-growth-mindset

Once you've completed the questionnaire, tally your total score and review your results based on the descriptions at the end of the worksheet

2

PLANNING

Probably one major thing to do before you commence with this project. Planning is the basis for any undertaking. One of the major tasks of an entrepreneur is to plan where the business should go in the future and devise ways on how to get there.

An entrepreneur has to determine the direction the business has to take. Planning is the starting point of any project, in this context the business project that you are starting or growing as an entrepreneur.

SMART goals

Setting goals, developing milestones (plans) to reaching those goals and the implementation of the plans are all the steps in this planning process. It is often said that, if you fail to plan, you are planning to fail. A SMART criterion is a technique used for setting effective goals. Goals set should be; Specific, Measurable, Attainable, Realistic and Time bound (SMART).

Brainstorming

Brainstorm your ideas to generate multiple alternatives and perspectives and ultimately funnel it down to the few best. You can do this with a group of friends, family or business partners. The premise is to choose the best idea that you will adopt moving forward.

Few ideas on what you can base your brainstorming session on:

- Creative name generation and search for your entity
- Is there a need for your anticipated products/services?
- Who needs it (customers)?
- Are there other companies offering similar products/services now?
- What is the competition like?
- How will your business fit into the market?
- Are there opportunities for growth?

These are perhaps some of the questions and more that you will have to answer during your brainstorming sessions.

Research

In this section, you will have to find out information, conduct miniature literature survey on the industry that you would like to form part of. Things such as challenges and opportunities in that particular industry need to be identified or SWOT analysis. An analysis of the macro-and market environment and the positioning of the business in the market must be conducted - analysis of your business competition. You must also explain how you are different from your competition (USP). You don't need to say that you are better than your competition, but you should explain how your business is unique, and how it differentiates itself from competition.

Key skills and success factors you need as an entrepreneur

- Ingenuity - includes knowledge, skills, understanding of a business environment and industry, and creativity. Basically, ingenuity involves generation of new ideas.

- Leadership - good human relations and a positive attitude are the basis of leadership. A good leader is positive, well-adjusted, realistic, self-confident, group oriented and a team builder, who seeks solutions, motivates people, gives individual responsibility and gives credit for achievements.

- Calculated risk-taking - successful entrepreneurs don't take chances but sometimes they feel it is necessary to take calculated risks. They first determine what the risk entails by evaluating it themselves, for example, by doing the market research or feasibility (is it achievable?) and viability (is it practical?) studies and with the help of experts. The use of experts ensures objectivity and careful evaluation. Entrepreneurs calculate probable results before they make decisions (Strydom *et al*, 2015).

Software & Toolkits resources

Toolkits resources needed for this stage include note pads, coloured pencils, sticky notes and pens to document ideas and enhance creativity.

3

HANGING YOUR SHINGLE

Finally, you decided on turning that idea in your head into a business! Congratulations! Now it is time to step out and take charge of your destiny. It is time to register your business. The process of registering a business is different depending on the type or form of entity you are starting and how big it is and the state you live in. We will take you through the basics of how to get your business registered.

Registration, Domain Name

Registering a business name is part of the process of registering separate entities like LLCs and corporations, depending on the one you will choose. It is very important to create a formal business structure, bank accounts and liability separate from your personal life. After your idea generation, the next step is to come-up with a name because everything else depends on it. It is the foundation from where everything will emanate as you build and grow your business. Decide on a location, it can be your home or rented home space. You will need this as your address for tax filings, bank account information and for important governmental departments' documents. Whatever name you come up and choose, ensure that it is not used by any other persons/business to avoid unnecessary litigation. Choosing a name, registering and possibly trade marking it means you have made a commitment to that name and it will stick with you forever.

Therefore, this is an important decision to make as an entrepreneur.

A domain name is not just an internet address where people can locate your business on the internet, it is more than that. It is an online identity of your business – meaning it will stick with your business forever. As a result, choosing a domain name for your business requires some brainstorming, considerable thought and thorough information survey (research).

Domains are easy and cheap to register and you can use Mailchimp – which you can use to unite your website, email, and landing pages under one recognisable name. You can also use GoDaddy to get a domain name and set up Wordpress there for free.

How do you find your domain name?

There are three (3) main parts to the domain name, namely; a domain name, an extension and an optional sub domain

1. Domain name – preferably use your company's name if you already have it. It makes it easier for people to make connection between your business and website. Ensure that you keep your domain name short and easily readable, avoid slang and don't include numbers or

hyphens.

2. An extension – this is the suffix at the end of the web address. Different suffix exists such as;

    - .org: If you run a non-profit, this will help distinguish you from a for-profit company
    - .info: Try this extension if you're only using your site to share information
    - .biz: Got an e-commerce site? This is a good alternative to .com
    - .net: A good option if you're in the tech industry

Try to get .com simply because it is a popular one and easy to remember but it is not the only one as shown above. You might have to choose the one fit for your business.

3. Optional Sub-domain - this is the http://www. starting of part of your website

After choosing the domain name that you are happy and satisfied with, the next step is to register it. You can register you domain name with Mailchimp, they give you an option to search for a domain for free and you can purchase it right from your account. When you purchase a domain through Mailchimp they automatically generate SSL certification and WHOIS privacy making it easy to create a secure website experience for your business. Or you can use GoDaddy to purchase and register your domain. After all this is done, now you can put your domain name to use to market your business and push your brand out there.

Your website & social media

Building a website is like building an online home for your business. You can use Mailchimp where you can use their new drag and drop website builder to design and publish your site. You can also use your domain name for social media handles but check for availability first. A unified brand name and identity across allplatforms can help increase your reach. Make sure you choose social media handles that make it easier to connect with your brand or name.

Setting up your emails

Setting up your professional email address is part of building your brand online. As you continue to build your brand and put it before potential audiences, you can do this by using Google Workspace to create your email address using the domain name you have already chosen. Sending emails from a professionally created email address helps to build trust with your customers from the start. Using Google Workspace gives you access to tools like Google Drive, Sheets, Docs and Slides that makes it easier to develop documents to interact with your employees and potential customers.

Your Mission & Vision

It is important to outline your mission statement which is the definition of your entity's basic business scope and operations that differentiate it from similar typesof businesses. A mission statement is your purpose – your reason for existence. Your vision on the other hand is future-oriented. It is an outline of where you would like to see your company in the future.

4

LAYING AND FILLING THE FOUNDATION

Branding & logo design

One of the most important decisions that you will have to make based on the nature of the product is the choice of your brand. Your brand becomes your identity. This helps you to distinguish your products from those of your competitors. It includes a brand name and a specially designed trademark or logo. In today's highly competitive markets, it is impossible to market your products successfully without brand identification. Your distinctive name and trademark/logo are often used in reminder marketing. Examples of popular brand names such as Apple, BMW, Mercedes Benz, Nike are easily recognisable.

Choosing stock marketing images

Need free images to use for your website design and other stuff such as social media posts and ads! You can get access to over 2 mil stock photos using Unsplash and others. You can use Canva for your social media posts.

Setting up file systems & backup

Set up file systems and important document backup for your business. Tools such as Google Drive and Dropbox can be useful.

5

FINISHING THE FOUNDATION

Useful Software & Systems

It is useful to establish your software and systems in order to grow your business in a sustainable manner. Establish processes earlier on so that you can be efficient and scale your business. No matter how small your business is, you need project management and tools to be able to track projects for you and your team. It is critical to automate your processes which you use to run your business so that the business will run on its own and you can focus on other things to grow.

Below are some of the tools and processes.

- Trello
- Bitrix
- Canva
- Zoom United (unified app for meetings, phone & chat)
- Kajabi

- Loom Mindmaster

Hiring

As an entrepreneur, when you start-off you are faced with a challenge of limited resources so you will be expected to wear different hats. You are the owner, marketing manager, administrator, accountant etc. However, as the business grows and expands you can hire external expertise and add more human capital.

Basic Marketing

The all important marketing plan and promotion of your business. You must be able to promote your business and get customers. Without marketing and without clients, a business can't survive for long so your marketing plan is absolutely important. It isn't enough just to have any old marketing plan. The marketing plan explains how the products or services will be brought to the attention of the consumers and where they will be able to get them. Your marketing plan must be very good and savvy. If your current marketing plans consist of promoting on Facebook, Twitter, with business cards and flyers, you must definitely come up with a more professional marketing plan.

The main objective of a business is to maximise profitability in the long run. It is generally recognised that marketing is central to this objective because of its role in defining customer needs and wants, and directing the resources of the business to meet these needs and wants. Promotion entails communication methods that can be used such as competitions, demonstrations, rewards based system and handing out samples in trying to influence consumer behaviour. Promotions often have short-term objectives only, to introduce a new product to the market.

6

HITTING YOUR STRIDE

Lead generation & CRM

Lead generation is how you get customers. Different methods of capturing leads include landing pages and websites to collect data and build an email list of your customers and prospects. It is overwhelming sometimes to know which systems to choose and use when starting a business or to grow it for that matter. Get your customer relationship management tool to help you make sales, track your customers and for fulfilment of those orders. So which to one choose? It depends on your product offering. Tools such as: Kajabi, Shopify, Close, Square etc.

Word of Mouth

Word of mouth in whatever form will continue to be important in marketing and driving sales. It is a form of referral that is worth noting. Presently, people around the world use social media platforms in its various forms (e.g. news feeds of Facebook and Twitter, private messaging on Whatsapp and WeChat and discussion forums on Reddit) for a number of reasons. This includes for the purpose of digitally communicating and socialising with friends and families, doing the same but with unknown others but who share common interests and accessing and contributing to digital content such as news, gossip and user- generated product reviews. All of these are word of mouth in one form or the other and referred to as online word of mouth (WOM) in the current digital era. Digital media is a new way to retain existing customers and acquire new customers for your business.

7

GROWING YOUR BUSINESS

The Key to Happy Employees

The importance of employee involvement in the process of customer satisfaction through production of quality goods and services to the specifications required cannot be ignored. Connecting with your customers positively impact your employees in that they find their jobs meaningful and lead to higher retention rate in your business. Happy employees create happy customers. Happy customers lead to business growth. You need customers to buy your products and services.

How & When to Expand

The first thing is to determine how and what you are selling in order to scale your business. It is crucial to outline your products or services so that you can set concrete goals that will bring your business long term success and help you to stand out in your industry. Your product offering should be tied with aspirations of your customers and your overall goals – you want your offering to exceed your customers' needs expectations.

Problem Solving & Innovation

Timely problem solving and innovation should be at the centre of your business. Generation of new ideas, innovation and creativity should become an operational or business reality especially in the current climate where uncertainty is at all high. The current pandemic has accelerated the process of digital transformation across all business. Innovation and technology enable businesses to solve real problems and provide much needed solutions to people. It is evident that the digital economy will play an important role in the recovery of the global economy post covid-19. Timely intervention to deal with hotspots in your business leads to growth. When customers are happy, they will buy your product/service and you can achieve growth.

8

SETTING UP SOCIAL MEDIA

Types of social media

Roll out your social media. Different types of social media platforms exist, such as;

- Facebook
- Instagram
- Twitter
- YouTube
- Pinterest
- Linkedin etc.

Social media is fundamental for your business. Before choosing your social media handles to use, check the availability of your domain name because you want a unified name across all your social media which will help increase reach. You want to tie your social media handles to your brand. It is easier for your audience to find your brand everywhere it appears online when your domain name is similar to your social media handles. Once you have your handles, set up your account profiles in each of the platform you decide on. This is where you build relationships with your customers and prospects and keep them engaged. Building lasting relationships with your customers is worth more than money. It is valuable.

Facebook Ads

Every entrepreneur and business owner ultimate goal should be to launch and scale their online business successfully. Given the current business environment that has tremendously impacted businesses (big & small) adopting a new normal built on digital and internet ecosystem is not an option but a necessity. Facebook platform and Facebook Ads have the potential to grow your business faster and tremendously. Mastering Facebook Ads is a requisite to take your business to that level. Youtube is a fantastic resource with free tutorials on basics of how to create a Facebook Ad. It is a great start! Check out Youtube tutorials.

These are the guidelines and toolkits needed to get your business off-the ground. It really is that simple. I'm passionate about helping businesses grow and I would love to have a chat with you.

Let's connect on: entrepreneur@wellfinity.co.uk/chippi@wellfinity.co.uk

Or linkedin.com/in/mogomotsi-lekoko-b6273a1ab

Setting up a business checklist

Phase ONE

Idea

- Define key strengths and values
- Brainstorm on business industries
- Market research competitors
- Define USP and test the market
- Find one paying customer/ case study
- Test the market
- Document and create a blueprint
- Validate the idea
- Launch the product

Conception

- Come up with business name. Keep it brief & memorable. Less errors when typing.

- Search on godaddy.com for existing domains, lock onto one that doesn't exist. Pick out .com or .whereveryouare

- Cross reference with Government Company House. (For UK check rapidformations.co.uk for existing company names)

- Register the company

- Use the company registration number to register a business bank account (Check out tide.co for quick turnaround).

- Sign up with a payment gateway, select stripe.com

- Register with an accountant (For UK check https://www.byzpulse.co.uk)

Design & Visibility

- Define brand image. Colours, logo, merchandise. Get your vector files. Check out https://www.wellfinity.co.uk/folio/creative/

- Purchase a domain. Check out www.bluehost.com/track/wellfinity/

- Create your business email addresses, hosting

- Create social media accounts, main ones Linkedin; Facebook; TikTok; Twitter; Medium; Instagram; Pinterest

- Remember uniform usernames across all platforms
- Create a liinks.co and add your top links into here
- Create a Google account, create a Google form with the onboarding questions for your product
- Embed this link into your enquiry email, web email and in outreach
- Remember to include source tracking

ABOUT THE AUTHOR

Mogomotsi Lekoko is an academic, author, scholar with over 10 years experience in the higher education sector. He is an experienced researcher with international publications spanning from entrepreneurship, entrepreneurial leadership, entrepreneurship education to small business development and business management. He has a Master's Degree in Entrepreneurship, Bachelor's Degree in Management and PGCHE which is a certification for professional educators. Heis currently a Head of Research & Development at Wellfinity LTD & Director at Wellpod.

Ashwin Sunassee is a founder & CEO at Wellfinity LTD & Wellpod, an entrepreneur and a philanthropist. He helps thought leaders and premium service providers increase revenue. He has over a decade of experience in the lifestyle and wellness sector, as well as an eye for detail and efficiency. He has particular skills in tailoring products and services to client needs and expectations, as well as extensive experience in marketing and contract negotiation with multinational corporations. His experience and on-going commitment to the third sector workingwith charities and community interest companies reflects a commitment to socially responsible and ethical business practices.

www.ingramcontent.com/pod-product-compliance
Ingram Content Group UK Ltd.
Pitfield, Milton Keynes, MK11 3LW, UK
UKHW020421250726
13967UKWH00007B/2756

9 781838 138677